DEVELOPING DIGITAL AND MEDIA LITERACY SKILLS

Digital Literacy: What Is It and Why Does It Matter?

Stephen Currie

San Diego, CA

About the Author

Stephen Currie is the author of dozens of books for children and young adults, including *Sharing Posts: The Spread of Fake News* for ReferencePoint Press (2017). He has also taught grade levels ranging from kindergarten to college. He lives with his family in New York's Hudson Valley.

© 2024 ReferencePoint Press, Inc.
Printed in the United States

For more information, contact:
ReferencePoint Press, Inc.
PO Box 27779
San Diego, CA 92198
www.ReferencePointPress.com

ALL RIGHTS RESERVED.
No part of this work covered by the copyright hereon may be reproduced or used in any form or by any means—graphic, electronic, or mechanical, including photocopying, recording, taping, web distribution, or information storage retrieval systems—without the written permission of the publisher.

LIBRARY OF CONGRESS CATALOGING-IN-PUBLICATION DATA

Names: Stephen, Currie, author.
Title: Digital Literacy: What Is It and Why Does It Matter?/ by Stephen Currie.
Description: San Diego : ReferencePoint Press, 2023. | Series: Developing digital and media literacy skills | Includes bibliographical references and index.
Identifiers: LCCN 2023016193 (print) | ISBN 9781678205348 (library binding) | ISBN 9781678205355 (ebook)
Subjects: Information technology--Juvenile literature

CONTENTS

Introduction   **4**
Digital Literacy

Chapter One   **8**
Making Sense of the Digital World

Chapter Two   **19**
Fake News and Misinformation

Chapter Three   **31**
Scams, Attacks, and Hazards of the Digital World

Chapter Four   **42**
Oversharing and Online Privacy

Source Notes	53
For Further Research	58
Index	60
Picture Credits	64

INTRODUCTION

Digital Literacy

Each month millions of internet users read articles originating from satirical news sites, such as the Onion, the Babylon Bee, and the Borowitz Report. Though these websites are designed to look like the sites of mainstream news organizations such as ABC News or the *Washington Post*, they are not to be taken seriously. Instead of reporting the news, these sites include articles meant to parody it. Typical satirical news articles include the Onion's article "High Cost of Childcare Forcing More Toddlers to Work Their Way Through Preschool"—which quoted a fictional researcher lamenting that "the costs of snacks and picture books have to come out of [children's] own pocket"[1]—and the Babylon Bee's story about the state of the American banking industry headlined "Banks Begin Calling Customers to Ask for Loans."[2]

To some observers, the notion that anyone might mistake these tongue-in-cheek articles for real news is laughable. "The [Babylon] Bee is obvious satire," sums up journalist David French. "Obvious."[3] But over the years, many people have indeed taken stories from satirical sites at face value. Near the end of the 2020 presidential campaign, for instance, then-president Donald Trump was taken in by a Babylon Bee item claiming that Twitter had shut down to ensure that people did not spread negative stories about Trump's opponent, Democrat Joe Biden. "Wow, this has never been done in history," Trump wrote. "Why is Twitter doing this[?]"[4] And Trump is not alone. A 2019 study asked Americans to determine whether certain satirical news items were true or false. In multiple cases, more than 10 percent of respondents categorized stories as "definitely true." The study's authors summed up their findings by saying, "Too many people think satirical news is real."[5]

> "High Cost of Childcare Forcing More Toddlers to Work Their Way Through Preschool."[1]
>
> —Headline in the satirical website the Onion

The difficulty many people have in identifying satirical news exemplifies the need for digital literacy. Though experts disagree about the specific meaning of the term *digital literacy*, it usually refers to a variety of skills, including the ability to find content online, create digital content, communicate digitally, and—perhaps most important—evaluate what is found online for accuracy and trustworthiness. As journalist Liana Loewus sums it up, digital literacy encompasses "everything from reading on a Kindle to gauging the validity of a website or creating and sharing YouTube videos."[6]

Digital Literacy and Critical Thinking

At first glance, it might seem that today's youth would be highly digitally literate. After all, the teenagers and young adults of the 2020s were brought up in a world of texts, social media sites, and online games. They have used laptops, tablets, and smartphones since they were small children, and they are adept at shopping online, creating and sharing posts on social media sites such as TikTok, and using search engines to find anything and everything. Indeed, their familiarity with technology has led some observers to call them digital natives. "Digital natives have grown up with internet access, depend heavily on mobile devices, heavily consume social networking services . . . and multitask across devices and between work and entertainment,"[7] notes a publication of the American Library Association. Skills such as uploading videos, texting, and installing apps on smartphones are second nature to younger Americans today.

Despite these talents, even the most heavily wired teenagers and young adults may lack important digital literacy skills. The

5

difficulty many Americans have in determining whether stories from the Onion and the Babylon Bee are genuine news articles points to part of the problem. The ability to maneuver one's way around the internet is a practical skill, not one that generally requires critical thinking. Familiarity with cyberspace is of little help when it comes to the more serious questions of which websites to trust, how to avoid online scams and predators, how to avoid posting information that could be embarrassing, and how to make sense of the enormous amount of information available online. The sad truth is that even people who have never known a world without digital devices and social media can still be tak-

Today's youth have grown up with electronic devices and are very good at using them. Despite this, they often lack important digital literacy skills.

en in by online swindlers, regularly post too much information in cyberspace, and have difficulty distinguishing good information from bad. No matter a person's familiarity with the digital world, these are critical-thinking skills that must be taught.

Fortunately, many available resources can help build essential digital literacy skills. Many high schools and colleges, along with national organizations such as the American Library Association, offer information to internet users wondering whether a website is reliable. Similarly, government agencies provide tips on how to avoid being swindled on the internet, and psychologists and other scientists have recommendations designed to help people think before they post. As a result of these resources, everyone can become digitally literate. The trick is to pay close attention to what these resources say—and follow through by taking their advice.

CHAPTER ONE

Making Sense of the Digital World

The amount of information that can be found in cyberspace today is mind-boggling. The number of YouTube videos available online as of early 2023 has been estimated at 800 million, or approximately one video for every ten people in the world. Facebook posts, in the meantime, number in the trillions. Google searches for the most esoteric of topics bring up hundreds or thousands of websites, while searches for more popular or controversial subjects can bring up millions. Looking up the term *digital literacy* on Google, for example, leads to over 300 million results, from newspaper articles and university websites to government publications and corporate blogs. Similar numbers apply to searches for well-known personalities such as Beyoncé and Donald Trump. By some estimates, the world has produced more information since 2010 than in all of human history preceding it.

On one level, this is a good thing. Consider the ease with which people can access this information in a digital world. In the not-so-distant past, students who needed to know the population of Kansas in 1870, research the arguments in favor of solar energy, or identify the causes of World War I would likely have taken a trip to the library. There they would have consulted a card catalog or a bound index of periodicals to find appropriate sources—and then waded through books, magazines, and newspapers to come up with the information they needed. Today that same student needs only an internet connection and a minute or two to determine that 364,339 people lived in Kansas in 1870. Even learning about the causes of a war or the controversies regarding energy sources has become much easier than it was in the pre-digital days.

But the sheer number of websites (and blogs, podcasts, posts, and news feeds) can actually be an obstacle to digital literacy. The amount of information can be overwhelming. How can people determine which websites to access—and trust—when there are hundreds of millions of pages to choose from? Which emails need immediate attention, and which can safely be ignored until later? What are the emotional and physical effects of being connected to the internet virtually around the clock? These are all concerns in a wired world. Developing stronger digital literacy skills can help reduce the drawbacks of this information glut—that is, if people are willing to make some changes in how they approach the digital universe.

Good and Bad Information

The ability to distinguish good information from bad is a central skill for dealing with the overabundance of data on the internet. While many websites provide relevant and timely information about a given topic, others leave out important facts, are out of date, or are riddled with errors. Knowing which websites fall into which category is crucial. That is particularly true because of the ease with which information can be posted online. "Librarians and other experts pre-select materials available from the library," points out a library guide put out by Seminole State College in Oklahoma. "However, anyone can write and publish information [online]. . . . Websites in particular can be tricky to assess."[8]

In some cases it can be relatively straightforward to identify online information that should not be used. Websites may have a date that marks them as obsolete, for example. A student who is researching a paper about current controversies in the US Congress, say, has no use for an article with a publication date of 2005. Similarly, some websites look amateurish, with frequent misspellings, grammatical mistakes, and untidy layouts, and these sites too should generally be avoided. As a guide published by Western Kentucky University reports, poor design and the tendency to type in all capital letters "are often signs that information is not trustworthy."[9]

More often, though, it is difficult to tell which websites are trustworthy, unbiased, and up-to-date. Evaluating the value of these websites relies even more on digital literacy skills. Fortunately, experts have developed some useful guidelines to help internet users find appropriate websites. Websites all have domains, or suffixes—letters that follow the dot near the end of the address—and looking at the domain of the website's address can be helpful. The suffix ".gov," for example, is reserved for documents issued by the government. The vast majority of websites ending in ".gov" are likely to be reliable. Similarly, experts recommend looking for websites with the suffix ".edu," which denotes information put out by educational institutions.

There is a vast amount of information online. A Google search for a popular topic can return hundreds of millions of hits.

Too Much Online Interaction

Spending too much time in the digital world can have social ramifications as well as an impact on cognitive functioning. Many studies have identified impairments related to the in-person social skills of teenagers who spend much of their time online. Most researchers agree, moreover, that interactions on social media are much more complicated than offline social relations. Unlike real-world connections, points out Brown University psychologist Jacqueline Nesi, social media interactions are both public and permanent. An embarrassing post is available for all to see—possibly forever. "After you walk away from a regular conversation, you don't know if the other person liked it, or if anyone else liked it—and it's over," says Mitch Prinstein of the American Psychological Association. "That's not true on social media." Prinstein and others fear that overuse of social media sites, especially by youth, can have damaging effects on self-esteem, mental health, and social skills.

Quoted in Zara Abrams, "Why Young Brains Are Especially Vulnerable to Social Media," American Psychological Association, August 25, 2022. www.apa.org.

Most websites do not have ".edu" or ".gov" domains, however, and experts typically recommend viewing other domains with some suspicion. Nonprofit organizations often have ".org" suffixes, for instance, and while websites ending in ".org" can be very useful, they are not always reliable. "Analyze .org sites carefully," advises a guide to online research put out by Central Michigan University. "Many are biased toward a particular agenda they're pushing."[10] It can be important to understand what that agenda is and to check information presented on one of these websites against other sources. The same is true with websites ending in ".com," which typically include websites put out by businesses. A website belonging to a company that makes laptops, for example, may provide valuable information about electronic devices in general—or may function mainly as an extended advertisement for the company's products.

Once internet users have identified websites that look promising, they should ask themselves questions to help ensure that the websites are indeed trustworthy. Determining authorship, for

Some websites are more trustworthy than others. The ability to choose good sources is important for anyone who looks up information online.

example, can be important. "Does the article or study have any authors listed?" asks a research guide published by the University of Texas at El Paso. "If so, do they cite or link to authoritative sources, or are they writing their own opinions without backing them up with facts?"[11] Spot-checking facts and arguments by checking a different source is also a good idea. If a second source agrees with the first, that can be an indication that the first was reliable. The digital literacy skills involved in asking these questions will help internet users become increasingly better at making their way through the millions and millions of websites available to them.

Stress, Distraction, and Multitasking

The issues raised by the information glut, however, go well beyond developing the skills necessary to find reliable websites. The wired world in which the great bulk of today's Americans live affects humans both biologically and psychologically. Our brains are simply not designed to keep up with or process so much data. It is therefore extremely difficult for us to pay attention to the barrage of texts, emails, and instant messages we receive on a regular basis—to say nothing of the news items and human interest stories that bombard us via the internet each day. "We've all seen or experienced the case of 'I get too many emails to read them all,'"[12] writes the director of IQVIA Technologies, a global health science analytics and research services firm.

Indeed, many people complain that they have difficulty getting things done because of the electronic communication and entertainment options in the modern world. Studies show that more than half of office workers say they regularly experience distraction on the job, cutting their productivity and leaving them feeling frustrated. In a 2012 college commencement speech at the University of the Arts in Philadelphia, British writer Neil Gaiman lamented the sheer number of emails he responded to during times he had set aside for working. "There was a day," he said, "when I looked up and realised I had become someone who professionally replied to email, and who wrote as a hobby."[13]

The effect, all too often, is to pull us in several directions at once—making it difficult if not impossible for people to focus their attention on anything at all. "[This] state, commonly known as information overload, can have dire consequences," reports an IQVIA Technologies publication. People affected by information overload "often report an increase in stress levels, distraction, and delayed decision-making."[14] Stress is a particular problem. The American Psychological Association points out that in addition to leading to lower efficiency at work, at school, and in life, people who are experiencing psychological stress

> "There was a day when I looked up and realised I had become someone who professionally replied to email, and who wrote as a hobby."[13]
>
> —Author Neil Gaiman

have a greater chance of becoming physically ill. For example, health experts report, stress raises the risk that a person will contract heart disease, diabetes, and a host of other illnesses.

Many people attempt to lower the stresses of the digital era by multitasking—meaning trying to do more than one thing at a time. An office worker might try to field phone calls from clients while keeping an eye on a training video, for example. On the surface, multitasking seems like a sensible way to save time and energy. But experts argue that it is not. Indeed, scientific evidence suggests that multitasking is nearly impossible. Instead of concentrating on multiple things at once, people who try to multitask are in fact switching between activities in quick succession—a process that slows thinking and interferes with productivity. "The more we multitask, the less we actually accomplish," says neuropsychologist Cynthia Kubu. "We unequivocally perform best one thing at a time."[15]

Some experts have likened the experience of trying to pay attention to multiple digital stimuli to the symptoms of attention-

Cognitive Benefits and the Internet

While many researchers worry about the negative consequences heavy internet use may have on the brain, some studies call their concerns into question—or suggest that spending time online may carry certain cognitive benefits. Some scientists argue, for example, that our newfound ability to store information digitally is actually a net plus for the brain. Even though the internet seems to impair memory function, they assert, the parts of the brain no longer used for memory storage do not wither away; rather, they are now available for other, more complex cognitive tasks.

There is also evidence that under some circumstances, internet use can improve brainpower. One study of retired Europeans demonstrated gains in memory recall among those who used the internet compared to those who did not. "Using the internet, post-retirement, leads to a marked reduction in the rate of cognitive decline," sums up one of the researchers.

Quoted in Chia-Yi Hou, "Retirees Using the Internet Get a Boost to Cognitive Function," *The Hill* (Washington, DC), September 23, 2021. https://thehill.com.

deficit/hyperactivity disorder, or ADHD. Few scientists would argue that heavy use of the internet causes ADHD. Evidence generally suggests that ADHD is a neurodevelopmental disorder present from birth, rather than a condition that can be developed later in life. Still, there is evidence that the internet alters our ability to pay attention in ways reminiscent of the workings of ADHD. "The limitless stream of prompts and notifications from the Internet encourages us towards constantly holding a divided attention,"[16] says Australian researcher Joseph Firth.

> "The limitless stream of prompts and notifications from the Internet encourages us towards constantly holding a divided attention."[16]
>
> —Australian researcher Joseph Firth

Changes to the Brain

Indeed, the digital world may alter the brain itself in subtle but important ways. Attention is a good example. Several studies have associated heavy internet use with a reduction in the size of parts of the brain known to be involved in attentional control. "Our brain grows and changes based on our experiences," says University of Chicago psychologist Michael Pietrus. "Not only are we able to create new neurons and form new pathways, but our beliefs and actions can dramatically alter brain chemistry and composition." Pietrus argues that internet use can create symptoms that mimic ADHD in people who do not have the disorder—and make symptoms worse in those who already have it. "Our use of various social and online media can . . . affect our neurocognitive abilities, and contribute to functional impairments,"[17] Pietrus explains.

The glut of information on the internet may also be affecting our memories. In one study, participants were asked to type a list of facts into a computer file. Half were told their work would be automatically saved; the rest were informed that their work would be lost. Later, members of both groups were asked to recall as many facts as they could. Study subjects who believed their work would be saved performed significantly worse on this test than

Some studies suggest that frequent use of video games may physically alter the brain, although results are not conclusive.

those who thought it would not be saved. Apparently, we are offloading the responsibility of recalling data to our devices. This phenomenon is often called the Google effect, named for the tendency of people to have difficulty remembering information that can easily be found online. Some scientists worry that this loss of memory power may carry over to a similar loss of memory strength in areas beyond cyberspace. In other words, people will find it harder and harder to remember information they have learned, regardless of its source.

Frequent use of video games may also alter the brain, though researchers are divided on just how much and what the actual effects might be. While a recent study carried out by the National Institutes of Health, for one, suggests that video gaming may improve brainpower, other study results are less positive. A study in Lebanon, for example, found that the more hours preteen students spent playing video games, the more likely the students were to have learning issues. "Higher addiction to video gaming," the Lebanese research team reported, "was significantly associated with worse episodic memory, problem solving, basic reading skills, written expression skills, and . . . attention."[18]

Cutting Down on Distractions

The amount of information available in a digital universe takes the form of statistics, news items, social media posts, video games, and more. The available data has changed the way people do research, interact with each other, and think about the world. As indicated by rising stress levels, possible changes to the brain structure, and (largely unsuccessful) efforts to multitask, the overabundance of data is a problem with which the people of the twenty-first century must contend. How can internet users maximize the enjoyment and practical value of being online while avoiding the stress the digital world places on our bodies and minds?

The answer is straightforward, though not necessarily simple. The first step, experts suggest, is tracking internet use. People who spend large portions of their days online are advised to record the amount of time they spend on the web—and in particular, the amount of time they spend being distracted by pings, instant messages, checking TikTok, and so on. Tracking can be done in a physical notebook or by using an app. A program called RescueTime, for example, can be set to distinguish online time that is productive from online time that is spent on distractions. Many users of RescueTime and similar apps are surprised to learn just how much time they spend checking Snapchat or CNN on a daily basis.

The second step is to make an intentional effort to reduce those distractions. Neil Gaiman, for example, found a solution to the overabundance of emails he replied to: "I started answering fewer emails," he reports, "and was relieved to find I was writing

> "Internet-blocking apps have become a lifesaver. When I need to focus, it's a great relief to fire up a blocker, quiet the noise, and just get to work."[20]
>
> —Writer Christopher Curley

much more."[19] Some people deliberately turn off alerts or disengage from social media sites at times when intense focus is necessary—such as when writing a paper or studying for a test. Apps can be used to block certain websites altogether. People who find it especially difficult to ignore Snapchat notifications or breaking news pop-ups from CNN can simply install a program like Freedom or Cold Turkey Blocker to prevent access to those sites. "Internet-blocking apps have become a lifesaver," says writer Christopher Curley in an essay on Business Insider. "When I need to focus, it's a great relief to fire up a blocker, quiet the noise, and just get to work."[20]

From thinking uncritically about information posted online to the stress caused by trying to keep up with social media, the effects of massive amounts of information can lead to problems. Fortunately, these issues can be alleviated through digital literacy. People who are digitally literate stop to ask themselves whether information they find online makes sense—and where it comes from—before accepting it as valid or accurate. Similarly, people who are digitally literate know how to focus on just one task and how to take breaks when necessary. The reality is that the digital world is here to stay. Our task is to lessen the negative impact of time spent online.

CHAPTER TWO

Fake News and Misinformation

In December 2019 a highly contagious and often deadly virus made its first appearance in China. The coronavirus SARS-CoV-2 caused severe respiratory illness. The most vulnerable were older people and people with compromised immune systems, but people of all ages and circumstances became infected, and many died. The virus and the illness it caused—later given the name COVID-19—soon made its way from China to other countries. By the spring of 2020 it was clear that the disease was going to run rampant across much of the United States, with dangerous consequences for the population. "We're going to get hit," physician Anthony Fauci observed that March. Fauci, director of the National Institute of Allergy and Infectious Diseases at the time, added, "There's no doubt about it."[21]

Fauci was correct. Ordinary life was disrupted for months in the United States and beyond as COVID-19 raged across the planet. In hopes of containing or preventing the spread of the virus, companies closed their physical facilities, schools went to full-time remote learning, sports teams played in empty stadiums, and many governments required the wearing of masks in public while forbidding parties, parades, and other gatherings. Nonetheless, as Fauci predicted, the virus was not to be stopped. Estimates suggest that COVID-19 killed 3 million people worldwide in 2020 alone. In the United States COVID-19 was the third leading cause of death in

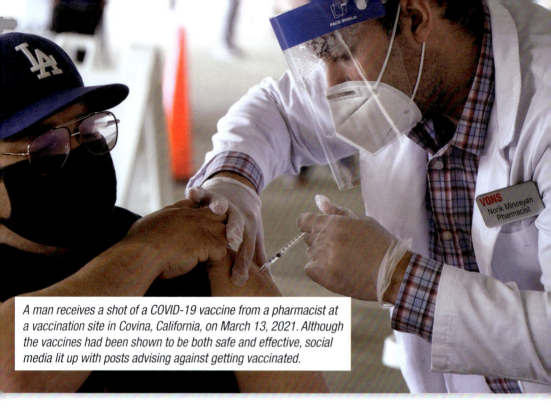

A man receives a shot of a COVID-19 vaccine from a pharmacist at a vaccination site in Covina, California, on March 13, 2021. Although the vaccines had been shown to be both safe and effective, social media lit up with posts advising against getting vaccinated.

both 2020 and 2021, ranking behind only heart disease and cancer. By March 2023, according to the Johns Hopkins Coronavirus Resource Center, 1.1 million Americans had died from COVID-19, and the global death toll had reached 6.9 million.

During those years, scientists worldwide spent many hours trying to understand the virus, the disease, and the best ways to prevent and treat it. But not everyone accepted the emerging science behind COVID-19. Many different narratives began circulating. Many people bought into those narratives. Fueled largely by social media posts, online videos, and the statements of various political leaders, these narratives spread quickly around the globe. Some websites claimed, falsely, that injecting disinfectant or swallowing ivermectin, an antiparasitic drug commonly used in the care of horses, would be effective against the coronavirus. Others incorrectly spread the word that COVID-19 itself was a hoax. "If we were in a real pandemic people would be dying in their homes by the thousands, hazmat teams would be removing bodies daily, [and] mass grave sites would be everywhere,"[22] argued one Facebook user in a post shared hundreds of times the first day it was up.

Nearly a year into the pandemic, vaccines finally became available. Although the vaccines had been shown to be both safe and effective, social media lit up with posts advising against inoculation. Many posters claimed, inaccurately, that the vaccines did not protect people from COVID-19. Some went further, asserting that the vaccines infected recipients with other diseases, inserted minuscule robots into patients' bodies, caused infertility, or permanently altered the recipient's DNA. These and other false claims continued to circulate even in late 2022, as Philadelphia emergency room physician Anish Agarwal noted when he said, "We battle [these beliefs] every single day."[23]

Erroneous beliefs such as these, which spread quickly via the internet, are often referred to as misinformation or fake news. From early in the pandemic, scientists recognized that fake news about COVID-19 was a serious concern. They knew that the spread of misinformation about the virus worsened the situation by casting doubt on the pronouncements of physicians and researchers. The more people who bought into falsehoods regarding the virus, the longer and more destructive the pandemic would be. But at times the misrepresentations about COVID-19 seemed unstoppable. "We're not just fighting an epidemic," warned Tedros Adhanom Ghebreyesus, director-general of the World Health Organization, "we're fighting an infodemic. Fake news spreads faster and more easily than this virus, and is just as dangerous."[24]

> "We're not just fighting an epidemic, we're fighting an infodemic. Fake news spreads faster and more easily than this virus, and is just as dangerous."[24]
>
> —Director-general of the World Health Organization Tedros Adhanom Ghebreyesus

Politics and Entertainment

Fake news predates the internet. People have been circulating false rumors, conspiracy theories, and outright lies for years. Often these falsehoods are spread to support a political agenda.

21

MisinfoDay

Illinois and New Jersey are at the forefront of states that are bringing digital literacy into the classroom, but legal requirements are not the only way to teach students to recognize fake news. In Washington State, for example, the University of Washington hosts a one-day event for high school students and their teachers that focuses on media literacy. Known as MisinfoDay, the event includes workshops and other activities designed to make students better consumers of media products. Several hundred students attend MisinfoDay each year. The founder of MisinfoDay, University of Washington professor Jevin West, has been in contact with educators in other states and countries who are interested in his ideas. For West, programs like MisinfoDay are critical for helping students and others grapple with fake news. "Maybe eventually, some-day, nationally here in the United States," he says, "we will have a day devoted to the idea of media literacy. There are all sorts of things we can do in terms of regulations, technology, in terms of research, but nothing is going to be more important than this idea of making us resilient" where misinformation is concerned.

Quoted in David Klepper and Manuel Valdes, "Digital Literacy: Can the Republic 'Survive an Algorithm'?," AP, March 20, 2023. https://apnews.com.

Trying to capitalize on anti-Jewish sentiment of the time, President Franklin Roosevelt's detractors spread false stories that he was Jewish. Hoping to foment opposition to Abraham Lincoln's presidency during the Civil War, opponents circulated rumors, also false, that he had African American ancestry. These and other lies appeared in the popular press of the day. In 1898, for example, newspaper publisher William Randolph Hearst printed fake news stories and images intended to get Americans to support a war with Spain. Hearst's motives were in part to justify American expansionism, but as the owner of a media outlet, he had an economic motivation for the lies as well. "War makes for great circulation,"[25] he said.

But fake news in the nineteenth and twentieth centuries had a much more limited impact than it does today. That is largely because the realities of communication have changed dramatically.

In the information age, it is nearly as easy to send a message to a thousand people as it is to send it to half a dozen. Moreover, communication in the digital age takes place almost instantaneously, an enormous contrast from the days of Lincoln, Hearst, or Roosevelt. And communication in modern times is cheap: sending a hundred texts or emails costs practically nothing. Once, only wealthy newspaper publishers like Hearst could spread their ideas to millions of their fellow citizens. Today the combination of low prices, quick messaging, and ease of communication gives everyone with a smartphone even wider reach than Hearst had.

The most famous examples of fake news are political. These examples are designed to drum up support for a candidate or party or embarrass the other side and call its competence, integrity, and patriotism into question. A recent example is the QAnon conspiracy theory. In the words of an adherent, US representative Marjorie Taylor Greene of Georgia, QAnon holds that society is run in large part by a "global cabal of Satan-worshiping pedophiles,"[26] including many leaders of the Democratic Party. Though there is no evidence whatever to support this idea, QAnon has been accepted by many far-right conservatives. Another well-known piece of misinformation widely circulated on the internet is that the 2020 presidential election was actually won by incumbent Donald Trump and that Joe Biden's apparent victory was the result of fraud. Numerous vote recounts in states around the country have confirmed Biden's victory, postelection audits have found no evidence of widespread fraud, and dozens of court cases challenging the election have been dismissed for lack of evidence or for other reasons. And yet a Monmouth University poll taken in the fall of 2022 revealed that about 60 percent of Republicans erroneously believe that the election was stolen from Trump.

Other fake news items focus not on politics but instead on the entertainment or sports worlds. False rumors of celebrity deaths, in particular, can spread rapidly around the internet. "One month after the death of her son," read the somber title of a YouTube video posted in January 2023, "Rock 'n' Roll Queen Tina Turner

23

Convinced by fake news that the 2020 presidential election was rigged, angry Trump supporters storm the US Capitol on January 6, 2021.

suddenly passed away."[27] But while Turner's son did die in December 2022, Turner herself was alive and well as of March 2023. Other celebrities whose deaths have been erroneously reported in recent years include musician Kid Rock, professional wrestler Jey Uso, and Olympic sprinter Usain Bolt. When the announcement of Bolt's supposed passing was shared on Facebook in early 2023, nearly 1 million social media users responded to the message; most of them believed the story without reservation.

The Role of Social Media

Fake news websites are often difficult to distinguish at a glance from mainstream media sites. Website owners can use easily available technological tools to build sites that look professional. Many fake news sites, moreover, have addresses that differ only subtly from those of legitimate news providers such as CNN, the

Washington Post, or National Public Radio. But in one sense it is not necessary for fake news creators to spend much time on site design or even on the specifics of the stories. That is because the heart of a fake news article typically lies in the headline. Visitors to the site may not bother to read the article itself before sharing it with friends, relatives, and acquaintances online.

And once the article—or the headline—has reached a social media site, it will likely continue to be shared with others, regardless of what the story actually says. One recent study suggested that about six in ten Facebook users share articles without opening links that lead to the stories. As the headline of an article in *Forbes* magazine puts it, "59 Percent of You Will Share This Article Without Even Reading It."[28] The key, especially for political items, is simply that the headline match the reader's view of the world. A social media user primed to believe the worst about the Republican Party, for example, is likely to assume that almost any negative story about Republican leaders is accurate. The user then passes the story along without pausing to ask whether the article is adequately sourced or whether the story makes sense.

Indeed, the fundamental problem with fake news is its popularity among social media users. Multiple scientific studies have demonstrated that fake news items frequently draw more online views than do legitimate news articles. A team of American and French researchers, for example, examined the information available on Facebook before the 2020 US presidential election—and found that items originating with publishers of fake news were liked six times more often than items from mainstream news media. In addition, the truth does not travel nearly as quickly as misinformation. Compared to actual news items, sums up researcher Sinan Aral of the Massachusetts Institute of Technology, "false news diffuse[s] significantly farther, faster, broader, [and] deeper in every category of information."[29]

Experts on fake news agree that spreading misinformation has serious negative consequences. Sometimes the effects of fake news harm individuals: no one knows how many people lost their lives to COVID-19 by choosing to accept misinformation about the virus, but the number is not negligible—as suggested by the fact that the unvaccinated are several times more likely to die from the disease than are the vaccinated. More broadly, fake news damages society. Having conversations when the two sides do not agree on the facts leads to dissension and discord. That is particularly true where politics and government are concerned. "Disinformation threatens democratic structures,"[30] warns fact-checking journalist Uschi Jonas.

Jonas's unease was borne out on January 6, 2021, when more than two thousand Trump supporters—convinced by fake news that the 2020 election had been stolen from their candidate—stormed the US Capitol in an effort to overturn the outcome of the vote. In the end, the insurrection failed. Still, the rapid spread of disinformation about the 2020 election shook the foundations of the nation. "We want the public to understand just how close we came to a different result [that is, the illegal reinstatement of Trump as president]," sums up US representative Pete Aguilar of California, "and that democracy was in danger."[31] There is no guarantee that a similar situation will not occur again.

Fighting Back

As indicated by the ease with which misinformation spreads, it can be difficult to fight back against fake news. Experts typically recommend that internet users exercise caution and critical-thinking skills when they encounter any news story, especially one that does not come directly from a trusted news source. This is a good way to develop digital literacy, and it is useful advice. "The most important step to take is to interrupt your own reflex of sharing posts that outrage you or resonate with your beliefs,"[32] suggests a library guide put out by SUNY Geneseo, a liberal arts college in New York State. The cycle of fake news relies heavily on people suspending their ability to evaluate information and sending along questionable articles as if they were factual. Thus, breaking that cycle requires people to ask themselves important

The Appeal of Fake News

Fake news is powerful because it is so often believed—and so often forwarded on social media. Traditionally, observers have argued that the appeal of fake news involves what is known as confirmation bias: we believe stories that match our worldviews and so send them on to friends and family. People, in short, suspend their critical-thinking facilities when they see an article that fits what they already accept to be true.

Several experts, however, argue that confirmation bias is only part of our willingness to accept fake news and send it on. The fact that misinformation is typically sent by friends plays a large role as well. Professor S. Shyam Sundar, for example, argues that people trust their friends more than they trust experts: whether an article rests on facts and interviews with knowledgeable people is not of much concern to most social media users. Another professor, Matthew Asher Lawson, says that fake news spreads from one friend to the next because people are eager to conform. "If someone in your online tribe is sharing fake news," Lawson says, "then you feel pressure to share it as well, even if you don't know whether it's false or true."

Quoted in American Psychological Association, "Americans Share Fake News to Fit In with Social Circles," March 9, 2023. www.apa.org.

questions about the reliability of their sources—such as whether the claim makes sense or whether the person who sent the information has been wrong before.

Another piece of advice, familiar to those who have learned to use digital literacy to identify trustworthy information in general, involves researching the origins of the item. "Consider the source," a guide published by St. Louis Community College recommends. "Click away from the story to investigate the site, its mission and its contact info."[33] Sites spreading fake news may offer a never-ending supply of articles with the same political slant or the same degree of implausibility. Similarly, when the mainstream media is ignoring a story, it is probable—though not certain—that the story is untrue. Just as digital literacy skills help internet users distinguish reliable sources from ones containing errors, they assist in telling real news from fake.

This advice has limitations, however. In today's polarized political climate, liberals and conservatives may not agree on which news outlets are reliable. Republicans tend to champion Fox News as an unimpeachable source, for example, while Democrats dismiss it as a purveyor of fake news. It can also be difficult and time consuming to research the origins of a piece of potential misinformation. That is especially true if the item in question was received via social media with the original publication details stripped away. For this reason, internet expert Joe Carrigan recommends avoiding social media altogether when looking for news. "People should not get their news from social media—period," Carrigan says. "View any news content on social media with skepticism, and hesitate before you send it."[34]

> "People should not get their news from social media—period. View any news content on social media with skepticism, and hesitate before you send it."[34]
>
> —Internet expert Joe Carrigan

Schools and Libraries

The role of schools and libraries in the struggle against fake news is important as well. In the summer of 2021, Illinois governor J.B. Pritzker signed a law mandating that high schools in his state offer classes in media literacy. Though these courses were also designed to cover print media, the primary focus of the bill was on digital literacy. The new law is meant in large part to develop students' ability to identify erroneous information online and assess the credibility of sources on the internet. Much of the impetus for this bill came from Braden Hajer, a high school student from the Chicago suburbs. "I have seen firsthand what misinformation can do," Hajer told a reporter, referring to a friend who had fallen for several online conspiracy theories. "Thankfully, he pulled himself out," Hajer added, "but that was a rough few years."[35]

In early 2023 New Jersey governor Phil Murphy signed an even more extensive bill in his state. This bill not only required that New Jersey public schools offer what state officials called "information literacy" but mandated that every student in kindergarten through high school receive this instruction. "Our democracy remains under sustained attack through the proliferation of disinformation that is eroding the role of truth in our political and civic discourse," said Murphy upon signing the measure. "It is our responsibility to ensure our nation's future leaders are equipped with the tools necessary to identify fact from fiction."[36]

In addition to state governments and school systems, other organizations are acting to stem the spread of fake news and encourage media literacy. The American Library Association, FactCheck.org, and the National Association for Media Literacy Education are just three of the groups offering information to students, teachers, and others seeking to determine whether online

> "Our democracy remains under sustained attack through the proliferation of disinformation that is eroding the role of truth in our political and civic discourse."[36]
>
> —New Jersey governor Phil Murphy

High school freshmen work during a media literacy course at Brookfield High School in Connecticut on December 20, 2017. The course requires them to evaluate online sources for reliability.

posts are genuine or fake. A California nonprofit called the Center for Media Literacy, for example, provides schools with a MediaLit Kit—materials to help teach students how to maneuver though media, especially online, and tell fact from fiction. Other organizations have issued special reports on the problems presented by a lack of digital literacy, along with guidebooks for librarians and others who want to address these issues.

And some news organizations and social media platforms are also working to raise awareness of the concerns raised by fake news. TikTok, for example, has established a policy requiring the removal of videos that provide erroneous information. Indeed, during a six-month period in late 2022, TikTok removed about 1 million videos that violated this policy. "We do not allow harmful misinformation on TikTok," writes a company spokesperson. "We work with experts in academia, civil society and our U.S. Content Advisory Council to develop policies and enforcement strategies, as well as support digital literacy initiatives for our community."[37]

What Is at Stake

The rise of fake news in recent years is not just an annoyance. Because misinformation's spread carries serious consequences for the survival of our system of government, it is essential for people to do whatever they can to identify news that is real and distinguish it from articles that are deliberate fakes. As Syracuse University professor Jeff Hemsley puts it, "If it turns out that the lie is sexier than the truth, then we're in danger of undermining our very democracy."[38] One of the most important uses of digital literacy in today's society, then, is to avoid the confusion of fake news with facts.

CHAPTER THREE

Scams, Attacks, and Hazards of the Digital World

In May 2021 an American woman named Laura Francis received a message on Facebook purporting to be from a man named Davidson Hodge. Hodge explained that he was a physician affiliated with the US military, and he told Francis that he was looking for love. Although he was much younger than the sixty-nine-year-old Francis, Hodge said he was interested in being with "somebody that was more mature"[39] than the young women he had previously dated. Over the next few months, Hodge courted Francis assiduously, texting her daily, placing frequent video calls to her computer, and sending her YouTube videos of romantic songs.

Hodge's efforts to woo Francis were successful. "I fell in love with his voice," Francis admitted later on. "He had the cutest laugh."[40] Certain things about the relationship made her slightly suspicious—the age difference, for one—but she put these concerns aside. Despite never having met in person—Hodge explained that he was in North Korea working on a secret military mission—Francis and her new love interest were soon talking about marriage. Hodge was charming and attentive, she said later, and seemed to care deeply for Francis and her well-being. "Don't you think you're worthy of being loved?"[41] she recalled him asking at one point when she expressed reservations about his motives.

That summer, however, Hodge began asking Francis for money. The first request was for a new cell phone to replace Hodge's own, which he claimed had been lost. Other requests soon followed. At one point, for example, Hodge asked Francis for more than $42,000 so he could buy her an engagement ring. Buying the ring, he told her, would release him from his military contract, but he was unable to access his funds to pay for it at that moment. He promised to reimburse Francis and sent her a copy of a bank statement linked to an account containing $3 million. Francis did as Hodge requested. When the engagement ring proved to be a cheap zirconium worth only a few dollars, Hodge blamed the military officials supposedly handling the transaction. Though she was skeptical, Francis decided to keep the relationship going.

That was a mistake. In reality, there was no "Davidson Hodge" working with the US military in North Korea. The man who communicated daily with Francis and earned her confidence was in fact a scammer intent on separating Francis from her money. From beginning to end, the story "Hodge" fed to Francis was faked. The bank statement was a forgery, the secret mission was an excuse to explain why he could not meet with Francis in person, and the promises to reimburse Francis were lies. But whoever he was, the scammer was remarkably successful. Over the course of many months, Francis sent him almost $250,000 — money earmarked for her daughter's inheritance. "I thought I was smarter than this," says Francis today, thinking back to the red flags she ignored. "But guess what? I wasn't."[42]

Scams and the Digital World

Scams such as the one that took in Francis have been common throughout history. One scam that predates the internet involves writing bad checks—that is, checks drawn on nonexistent accounts. Con artists would convince businesses and ordinary citizens to take the worthless checks in exchange for cash, making off with thousands of dollars before the victims realized that they had been scammed. Job recruitment swindles were likewise pop-

An Email from a Scammer

This is an excerpt from an advance-fee email received by staff at Southern Illinois University, Edwardsville.

Please I need your urgent assistance in securing a consignment (two trunk boxes) containing ($20,000,000), the funds are surpluses of several contracts executed by my department during a supply of MH (Military Hardware).

The consignment is presently in Amsterdam Schiphol Airport in the Netherlands, via a U.S Military Air & Surface Transportation Company (ADM Europa LLC). My desire and purpose is to have the (ADM Europa LLC) to deliver the funds to you for safe-keeping until I return back to the U.S mid-next year after my deployment.

If you receive this message please e-mail me immediately with a delivery address and your full contact information; the deal is 60/40 split (60% for me and 40% for you); I am not a greedy woman and I hope you will not double cross a struggling uniform single mother with 3 teenage children?

Once you receive the consignment ($20,000,000) take out your 40% ($8,000,000) and save my 60% ($12,000,000) for me until I return back to the U.S mid-next year after my deployment.

May God bless you as you extend your helping hand to the needy!

Quoted in Jeff Laughlin, "The Prince Is Back and He Still Needs Your Help Moving Some Money, Old Scams Are New Scams," IT Spotlight, Southern Illinois University, Edwardsville, March 15, 2021. www.siue.edu.

ular in the pre-digital world. In these scams, scammers accepted money from job seekers in exchange for promises to find them employment—promises that were never kept. Ponzi schemes, named for early twentieth-century swindler Charles Ponzi, are another example. These are get-rich-quick investment opportunities in which early investors are paid off by funds obtained from later investors—who receive nothing when the pool of investors is exhausted. Like countless other scams, none of these swindles relied on modern technology for success.

But to the delight of swindlers and to the detriment of victims, the internet has dramatically increased opportunities for scams. Indeed, attempts to scam Americans are at an all-time high. In 2001, when only about half of Americans had internet access, the Federal Trade Commission (FTC)—the organization charged with investigating frauds and scams such as identity theft—received about 325,000 complaints regarding con artists. By 2022, when more than nine in ten Americans were internet users, the number of complaints had ballooned to 2.4 million. A study carried out by the Better Business Bureau showed an 87 percent rise in online scams from 2015 to 2022. The amount of money lost in these scams is staggering. The same study reports that victims of con artists were defrauded of $8.8 billion in 2022 alone.

The increase in successful online scams is partly a result of poor digital literacy. As exemplified by Laura Francis, many internet users have difficulty evaluating whether the people they meet and get to know online are trustworthy. In retrospect, Francis says she should have paid closer attention to warning signs. Among other things, the bank statement the scammer showed her to prove he had millions of dollars was filled with typographical errors. The scammer's story that he was on a secret mission in North Korea, a dictatorship at odds with the United States, might have raised alarm bells for Francis as well. But she did not act on her concerns; her desire for love overrode her reasoning ability to assess the risk to her.

Scams involving romance, such as the one Francis fell for, are all too common. In the United States alone, about seventy-three thousand people—male and female alike—were victimized by scams involving love and dating during 2022. The amount of money lost by these unwitting victims because of these cons exceeded $1 billion. Though the overall number of victims of romantic fraud dropped slightly between 2021 and 2022, the cost to the victims rose: the billion dollars scammers collected in these

Many people search for love on internet dating sites—but sometimes the "love connections" they find are really scammers looking for money.

schemes was the highest total on record. As the FTC puts it, "Romance scammers tell all sorts of lies to steal your heart and money, and reports to the FTC show those lies are working."[43]

To victims of romantic fraud, the lies scammers tell often seem quite plausible. Though scammers say they are perpetually in need of money, their low cash flow is always the fault of a government bureaucracy, a payroll mishap, or a bank late with a promised payment. Similarly, scammers make up stories about why they cannot meet their targets in person: they are in the military or working abroad for a secretive company or spending most of their time on an offshore oil rig. When they do make plans to visit their targets, flights are canceled at the last minute, new work obligations arise, or unrest in the area makes a trip to the airport inadvisable. Sometimes the excuse leads to a new request for money. Scammers might lament that their luggage has been

> "Romance scammers tell all sorts of lies to steal your heart and money, and reports to the FTC show those lies are working."[43]
>
> —Federal Trade Commission, which investigates online fraud

delayed at customs, for example, but suggest that if the target pays a fee the problem might be solved. All too often, the victims of these scammers oblige.

Other Scams

Romantic scams prey on the lonely, but other cyberscams prey on the greedy. Perhaps the most famous online swindle today is one known as the advance-fee fraud, or the Nigerian letter scam. This scam has its origins in the pre-internet days. The target originally would receive a letter in the mail from a person asking for assistance with a transfer of money, especially from a foreign country—notably Nigeria—into the United States. Today the letter has been replaced by an email or a social media post, but the con remains the same. "A scammer asks for your help to get millions of dollars out of his or her country," explains the North Carolina Department of Justice website. "All you have to do is provide your bank account number so the funds can be transferred and you'll get a cut of the money."[44]

Of course, the scammer is not actually interested in transferring money into a US bank, let alone into a victim's account at that bank. In fact, the money will only flow in the scammer's direction. Once the author of the email has the target's bank account information, the account will inevitably be drained of funds. Swindlers using this method of conning victims also have other ways of getting money from their targets, such as by asking for payments up front to facilitate the movement of the money out of their country. In addition, they may be able to collect personal information that will lead to identity theft. The outcome of engaging with these scammers, in any case, is uniformly bad. "You'll have less money than you had before dealing with them," reports information technology specialist Jeff Laughlin, "and will never get the millions from the original solicitation."[45] As of 2021 the average victim of advance-fee scams lost about $2,500.

A more subtle kind of internet fraud is known as phishing. In phishing schemes, scammers send emails purporting to be from a bank or an organization such as Venmo or PayPal that deals with money. Recipients are cautioned that there may be a problem with their account, a problem that they are told can be quickly resolved by visiting a website linked in the email. They are then instructed to log on with their usual credentials. The website closely resembles the financial organization's website—but it is not the real thing. Instead, it is designed to capture passwords and account numbers, allowing scammers to take money from their victims. Careful inspection can usually reveal that the emails and websites are not from the companies they claim to be, but the forgeries are not obvious. Unfortunately, most experts report that phishing schemes are becoming more sophisticated and harder to detect.

Malicious software, or malware, represents another common online scam. In this type of fraud, scammers release a program onto a victim's computer, phone, or tablet. The program, known

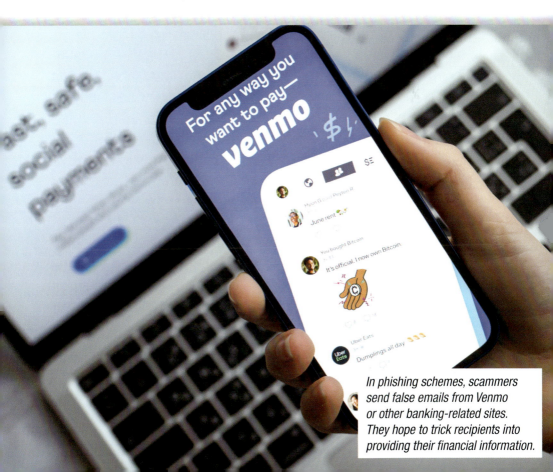

In phishing schemes, scammers send false emails from Venmo or other banking-related sites. They hope to trick recipients into providing their financial information.

as malware, is typically designed to collect personal information stored on the recipient's device. Malware can be distributed in various ways, including through phishing attempts, pop-up greeting cards, and attachments to email messages. Malware can also be spread through videos posted on social media sites. In 2022, for example, a powerful version of malware spread quickly through gaming communities by means of YouTube videos promising to help players master certain popular video games. Players of games such as *Spider-Man* and *Lego Star Wars* downloaded the offending videos, only to discover that they had been victimized by malware.

Predators

Though people regularly lose money when they fall for online scams, there are bigger hazards in cyberspace—some that have to do with personal safety. The main issue involves sexual predators who prowl the internet on messaging apps, social media sites, and chat rooms looking for potential victims. Most predators are adult men, and most targets—though not all—are teenage girls. Sexual predation online is alarmingly common. "One in five youth will be sexually solicited by an adult stranger online," reports psychology professor Elizabeth Jeglic, summarizing the results of a recent study, "and there is evidence that those numbers . . . increased during the pandemic."[46]

Some online predators start soliciting sex or nude pictures from a targeted teenager within a few minutes of making contact online. More often, though, predators move slowly, gradually winning the confidence of their victims by offering gifts, compliments, and a sympathetic ear. Even when the conversations remain nonsexual, though, predators caution their targets against telling trusted adults about what is going on. "Trust me, you are safe," typed one middle-aged Pennsylvania man to what he believed was a teenage girl (it was in

> "One in five youth will be sexually solicited by an adult stranger online."[46]
>
> —Psychology professor Elizabeth Jeglic

Sexual predators prowl social media, trying to lure young people—mostly girls—into inappropriate conversations and contact.

fact a police officer impersonating a child in hopes of catching predators). "This is our secret."[47]

When the conversation does turn to sex, the pressure can be difficult for victims to withstand. Predators are adept at making young people feel guilty about saying no—and at using threats to get what they want. When targets who have already sent nude or seminude pictures of themselves to the predator balk at meeting in real life, the predator may threaten to post the pictures in a public online forum—or send them to the victim's parents and friends. In some cases, too, predators threaten violence if their demands are ignored. As law enforcement agent Matt Wright explains, "They'll say, 'Here's your address—I know where you live. I'm going to come kill your family.'"[48]

Dealing with the Dangers

Whether the threat comes from phishing, sexual predators, malware, or something else, the internet can be a dangerous place

Online Shopping Scams

A very common internet scam involves online shopping. In a scheme reminiscent of phishing, fraudsters set up websites that look like the websites of legitimate stores and offer merchandise for sale. Customers are fooled into putting their credit card numbers into the websites, thereby surrendering their money and personal data. Of course, no items are ever delivered. These scams are becoming more and more frequent. As of 2022, online shopping scams represented the type of fraud most commonly reported to the Better Business Bureau.

In a similar con, swindlers also scour auction sites such as eBay to contact bidders who came close to winning an auction. "They will claim that the winning bidder pulled out or didn't have the funds," explains a booklet aimed at consumers, "and offer you the chance to buy the item." Bidders who agree are told to deposit their payment into a particular bank account—one which, needless to say, is not affiliated with the auction site itself. Again, buyers lose their money and compromise their credit cards without ever seeing the items they supposedly bought.

ScamWiseNI Partnership, *The Little Book of Big Scams*, 5th ed. London: Metropolitan Police Service, 2022. www.nidirect.gov.uk.

for unsuspecting users. Experts have plenty of advice to help people avoid being taken in by scams or criminal behavior. Most of their suggestions come down to vigilance, common sense, and the need to apply digital literacy skills. "If something sounds too good to be true, it probably is," notes the Kansas Attorney General's Office in a fact sheet directed at consumers. "Beware of offers for free products, claims you won a contest you did not enter, or get-rich quick schemes."[49]

Other advice deals with more specific situations. It can be possible to identify phishing scams, for example, by looking closely at web and email addresses. Does the web address look like a recognizable company's, only the company name is spelled incorrectly—with one letter too few or too many? All emails originating from the federal government in the United States have a ".gov" suffix; if an email says it is from the government but has a ".com" or ".biz" suffix instead, it is not genuine. Similarly, experts advise recipients of suspicious emails not to click directly on links given in the message. If recipients are not sure the email is genuine, but they do business with the company the email says it is from, the Federal Trade Commission advises consumers to "contact the company using a phone number or website you know is real—*not* the information in the email."[50]

Perhaps the best advice offered to avoid internet scams and attacks is simply to think things through. No matter how lonely for love a person may be, it is unwise for that person to send money to someone he or she only knows online. People asked to take part in an advance-fee scheme should ask themselves why they think the stranger who contacted them is trustworthy. Teenagers should be suspicious when a new internet friend—especially one from a different age group—takes a sudden interest in them, and especially when they are asked to keep the relationship a secret from parents and other adults. "Ask yourself, 'Does this make sense?'"[51] advises journalist Susan Tompor.

> "If something sounds too good to be true, it probably is. Beware of offers for free products, claims you won a contest you did not enter, or get-rich quick schemes."[49]
>
> —Kansas Attorney General's Office

In the end, protection from internet scammers and predators comes down to digital literacy. To fully defend themselves against harm, digital users must develop the ability to evaluate the information they see and receive online. Those who take the time to think critically about the messages they receive and the people they encounter in cyberspace; those who listen to the warning signs going off in their brains; those who start from the assumption that they should be suspicious—these are the digitally literate internet users who are best equipped to protect their money, their bodies, and their self-respect in an online world.

CHAPTER FOUR

Oversharing and Online Privacy

During the summer of 2022, a thirty-six-year-old woman named Sanna Marin attended a party with friends in her native country of Finland. Marin enjoyed the event. "I danced, sang, and partied," she recalled afterward. Though she admitted that she engaged in these activities "in a boisterous way," Marin saw nothing amiss with her attendance. Indeed, Marin argued that her appearance at the party was her business and no one else's. "I have a family life, I have a work life and I have free time to spend with my friends," she said. "Pretty much the same as many people my age."[52]

Had Marin been an ordinary citizen of Finland, her presence at the party would likely have escaped notice, let alone criticism. But she was not an ordinary citizen. Instead, she was the country's prime minister. A few days after the party, someone—it is not clear who—obtained videos of Marin singing, dancing, and drinking alcohol and posted them to social media sites. Before long hundreds of thousands of Finns had viewed the videos. The backlash was quick, with opposition party leaders questioning Marin's fitness to lead the country and demanding that she submit to drug testing. (Though Marin said she had not taken illegal drugs during the party, she did agree to a test; the results were negative.) "It's the PM's [prime minister's] bad judgment in the end,"[53] says Finnish journalist Tiina Lokka, just one of many critics of Marin's actions.

Marin survived the scandal. Though the incident was an embarrassment to her and her political party, she retained her position as prime minister, a post she continued to hold as of March 2023. Marin remains largely unrepentant. "I am going to be exactly the same person as I have been until now," she said, explaining that she had no plans to change her behavior, "and I hope that it will be accepted." What *did* bother Marin, though, was the posting of the videos online. Though she knew that the videos existed, she thought they would remain out of the public eye and was dismayed to learn otherwise. "I trusted that since the videos are private . . . they would not be published," Marin lamented. "It feels bad that they have been published."[54]

Although few people are as recognizable in their countries as Marin is in Finland, many of us can relate to the embarrassment that Marin suffered after having these videos appear on social

> "I trusted that since the videos are private . . . they would not be published. It feels bad that they have been published."[54]
>
> —Prime minister of Finland Sanna Marin

In 2022, videos were leaked online of Finland's prime minister, Sanna Marin (pictured), attending a rowdy party. The incident is a reminder that little remains private in the social media age.

media platforms. While there are wonderful things about the ability to share information, photos, and videos on sites like Twitter, Instagram, and YouTube, social media is not a place where preserving privacy is easy. People often post content that should not have been made public. An important part of digital literacy is the recognition that nothing that appears online is truly private, and another part is the ability to make a thoughtful decision about what information should—and should not—be posted on social media.

Oversharing and Celebrities

Determining what information to share online—and how much of it to share—is a question that comes up daily for internet users. For many people, the answer is to share as much as possible. From cat videos to pictures of vacations and from baseball scores to complaints about political leaders, the internet is flooded with images and information. The numbers are astonishing. According to Domo, an American software company, on average 500 videos were uploaded to YouTube every minute during 2022. Every minute, similarly, internet users post 66,000 photos on Instagram, send out 347,000 messages on Twitter, and share 1.7 million pieces of data on Facebook. "The volume and variety of [online] data keeps accelerating,"[55] Domo notes in an infographic titled "Data Never Sleeps."

The great majority of these Instagram photos and Facebook posts are harmless. But as Marin and countless others have discovered, some are not. There are many stories about people embarrassed or even humiliated by pictures they have posted—or in cases like Marin's, images and videos that others have placed online. Examples likewise abound of people who lost their jobs when they sent out tweets critical of their employers or were alleged to be active members of hate groups. Posting too often on social media can lead to problems with friends and family. The phenomenon of posting too much—or posting inappropriately—is sometimes called oversharing, and it can have serious consequences.

Oversharing and Burglary

Oversharing on social media can put internet users at risk of being burglarized. Many people like to show off expensive purchases such as jewelry, electronics, and bicycles by posting images of their new possessions online. However, law enforcement officials warn social media users that this practice is risky. Criminals have been known to look for pricey items in social media posts, often identifying the address through a victim's use of tagging, or identifying the location where a post was made. When they find items they like, they break into the owners' homes to steal the goods.

Security experts and police organizations, similarly, caution travelers not to post about their vacations until they return home. Again, would-be burglars can—and do—use this information to know when and where to break in. In a study from 2022, about 8 percent of British burglary victims were robbed on a day when they posted on social media from out of town. "We used to keep tabs on when [potential victims] were away from home," says an anonymous former burglar about criminals' use of social media. "We could find out where they were going and how long for, to plan the best way of making a move."

Quoted in Natalie Morris, "Ex-Burglars Reveal Common Social Media Posts They Use to Help Them Steal Your Stuff," Metro, February 1, 2022. https://metro.co.uk.

As psychologist Simon Boag puts it, "Oversharing is like a digital tattoo, a good idea at the time, but not always easy to get rid of."[56]

Oversharing is quite common in the digital world. Indeed, some people make their living in part by posting almost constantly about their lives. Video bloggers on YouTube, influencers on Snapchat, and reality television stars are all known for frequent social media posts. Celebrities such as Kim Kardashian, soccer star Cristiano Ronaldo, and singers Justin Bieber and Miley Cyrus post frequently to social media sites, where millions of followers read and view their thoughts and photos. Rapper Snoop Dogg, for example, averaged 647 social media posts per month in 2022—more than 20 a day. Some of these people, especially influencers, are paid to post on certain topics. Others find it financially beneficial to keep themselves in the public eye as much as possible.

Miley Cyrus attends the Tenth Annual LACMA Art & Film Gala in Los Angeles, California, on November 6, 2021. Cyrus and many other celebrities post frequently on social media.

The bulk of celebrity posts, like the bulk of posts made by members of the general public, are inoffensive. But some celebrities have run into serious trouble because of tweets they have sent and pictures they have posted. An early example took place in 2016, when singer Azealia Banks caused significant damage to her career after using racist and homophobic language to describe fellow singer Zayn Malik on social media. Undaunted by the backlash against her, Banks continued to post offensive material, attacking members of various nationalities and minority groups even as her agent abandoned her and her bookings diminished. According to one website, Banks "is now more known for her problematic social media presence than her music skills."[57]

Celebrities have not learned much from Banks's experience. In March 2023, for example, Memphis Grizzlies basketball star Ja Morant posted a video on Instagram in which he appeared to be carrying a firearm in a crowded nightclub near Denver. Morant's actions earned him a suspension and a police investigation into whether he broke Colorado's gun laws. (In the end, Morant was not charged due to lack of evidence.) The previous month, cartoonist Scott Adams, best known for the *Dilbert* comic strip, posted a video in which he made offensive comments about African Americans. In response, dozens of newspapers dropped *Dilbert*, and Adams's publisher abandoned plans to release a new book of *Dilbert* cartoons. "We will no longer carry [*Dilbert*] in the *Plain Dealer*," wrote the editor of the Cleveland *Plain Dealer*. "We are not a home for those who espouse racism. We certainly do not want to provide them with financial support."[58]

> "We will no longer carry [*Dilbert*] in the *Plain Dealer*. We are not a home for those who espouse racism. We certainly do not want to provide them with financial support."[58]
>
> —The editor of the Cleveland *Plain Dealer*

Jobs and Privacy

Celebrities may be especially prone to oversharing because they are so commonly at the center of public attention. But ordinary people have been hurt by oversharing as well. About 70 percent of employers check applicants' social media posts as part of the process of determining whom to hire. In some cases what they see causes them not to extend an offer—or to revoke an offer that was already made. In a 2023 case reported on advice columnist Alison Green's Ask a Manager website, a large company offered a managerial job to an applicant who had sent out tweets that one employee of the company called "blatantly racist, misogynist, and homophobic."[59] When the tweets were called to the attention of company administrators, the job offer was rescinded.

Other workers have lost existing jobs because of their social media posts. A Texas woman who had just found employment

Privacy and Harassment

In the summer of 2020, coaches of the Victory Vipers, a cheerleading team in Pennsylvania, received videos and photos via text that showed several members of their team drinking alcohol, vaping, or in various states of undress. The videos had been sent anonymously, and it was not at first clear whether they were real—or whether they were clever fakes. The case came to the attention of the police when the mother of one of the girls in the videos was sent what she described as threatening texts, again anonymously.

In fact, the cheerleaders had taken the videos themselves and posted them to TikTok and other social media sites. They thought the posts would remain private. They were wrong. Raffaela Spone, the mother of another member of the Victory Vipers, obtained access to the videos and sent them to the coaches and the cheerleaders' parents. The cheerleaders were removed from the squad, but Spone did not escape punishment for her actions. Under a Pennsylvania law that allows cyberbullying charges to be filed even if the victims did not receive messages directly from the bully, Spone was convicted of harassment in 2021.

at a day care center was fired almost immediately for posting the comment "I just really hate being around a lot of kids"[60] on Facebook. Other workers have been fired for disparaging their employers online, posting about engaging in illegal activities, or distributing confidential information such as the names of a company's clients or the salaries of employees. In a case from 2022, two teachers working in the same Arizona school district filmed sexually explicit videos of themselves on the grounds of the school where one of them taught. Then they posted the videos to several social media sites, including at least one that was not password-protected. Both lost their jobs.

Job loss is only one possible outcome of oversharing on social media. Privacy loss is also a concern. Any piece of personal information that appears on social media can present problems for the poster or the subject of the post. Identity theft is a particular risk. IdentityForce, an internet security company, notes that many people like to post pictures of updated driver's licenses. This is a bad idea. "While your best friend is admiring how good you look," an article on an IdentityForce web page points out, "identity thieves are thrilled that you just posted your name, address, birthday, and driver's license number."[61] Perhaps unsurprisingly, social media users run a considerably higher risk of falling victim to identity theft compared to people who avoid social media.

Interpersonal Issues

Oversharing can create interpersonal problems as well. Many social media users have had the experience of seeing photos from a friend's party on the internet and feeling hurt because they were not invited. In early 2023, for example, a letter writer described such a situation to etiquette expert Miss Manners. "Was it bad manners to post photos that people who were not invited to the party would see?"[62] the correspondent queried. Miss Manners agreed that it was indeed rude but acknowledged that the practice was extremely common. "A strict ban on such posts would bring social media to a halt,"[63] she noted in her response. Nonetheless, photos and videos taken at events from which others were excluded have the potential to cause rifts between family members and friends.

In the same way, people often post information or photos on social media that violate the boundaries and privacy of others. Social media sites are full of complaints from people whose friends or family members posted about them in ways that made them uncomfortable. "My friend posted an unflattering picture of me on Facebook,"[64] laments a Reddit user in a complaint seen over and over on social media. Some of these concerns can be easily resolved with a request to take down the offending post, but the requests are not always well received—and when they are, the post may already have been viewed multiple times. According to one study, almost 10 percent of social media users say they have ended a friendship because someone invaded their privacy by posting content about them without their consent.

In some cases, of course, social media users set out to cause harm. Cyberbullying, in which one or more participants deliberately harass another user through insults and hateful comments, is a major issue in the United States and elsewhere. But even when posts fall considerably short of cyberbullying, they can still cause damage. Many social media users have taken to Facebook, Reddit, or other sites to air their grievances with close friends or family members. Their intent may simply be to vent, but if the person being complained about happens to see the post, serious damage to the relationship may be the result.

The Permanence of Social Media

In one sense oversharing and loss of privacy are nothing new. Long before the rise of the internet, people were making cutting remarks directly to friends, grumbling to one family member about another, and gossiping about the personal lives of acquaintances. Similarly, people have complained for years about their bosses, and of course bigoted comments have been commonplace for generations. The speed, reach, and permanence of the internet, though, have dramatically changed the consequences of posting private information. An intemperate remark made directly to a friend in the pre-internet era, after all, would seldom have spread beyond a handful of people. Likewise, an unappealing photo appearing in a local newspaper would likely have been forgotten by most viewers within a week or two.

That is no longer the case. Today tweets and images can circle the globe in milliseconds. The videos showing Sanna Marin partying, Scott Adams disparaging Black people, and Ja Morant seemingly brandishing a weapon were immediately accessible to anyone in the world with an internet connection. Once content has been placed online, moreover, it is no longer controlled by the original poster. Instead, it can be passed from viewer to viewer in a seemingly endless chain—whether the poster or the subject likes it or not. Most people are aware of this possibility, and many are concerned that such an invasion of privacy will happen to

Gossiping is nothing new, but the rise of the internet has made it faster and easier than ever before to spread negative rumors about others.

them. According to a 2022 study, over half of social media users worry that someone will share their information against their wishes.

Of equal concern is the difficulty of making internet content disappear. "What you type floats around out there forever," one website reminds social media users. "And ever. And EVER. There is no permanent delete button."[65] Tweets critical of a coworker, embarrassing pictures of a neighbor, videos of intoxicated family members—all will likely be viewable online for years to come. In some cases the content creator can remove the offending post. But if the content has spread beyond the original poster, the process of deleting it becomes much, much harder.

Privacy vs. Oversharing

Internet users can avoid the traps inherent in oversharing by following some clear guidelines. Foremost among these is to be very aware of the realities of the internet. It is naive to believe that a post or video will remain private. "Assume what you share [online]

51

> "Assume what you share [online] can be seen by your friends, enemies, colleagues, boss, and another 5,000 people."[66]
>
> —Australian professors Van-Hau Trieu and Vanessa Cooper

can be seen by your friends, enemies, colleagues, boss, and another 5,000 people," say Van-Hau Trieu and Vanessa Cooper, Australian professors of information science. They also suggest that social media users think carefully about the words or videos they post. "Treat social media content like your personal brand," Trieu and Cooper advise. "If you wouldn't say it to your colleagues and managers, don't post it online."[66]

Other suggestions involve stepping away from the internet when frustrated or angry, especially when these feelings are aimed at a particular person. Studies show that people are more likely to make postings they will come to regret when they are in the throes of deep emotions. This finding should surprise no one who has experienced difficulty thinking clearly when upset. Some experts recommend taking long-term breaks, or even abandoning social media altogether if sites like Twitter and Snapchat begin to take over a user's life. "No one has to be on social media if they don't want to," says marketer Meredith Kallaher. "You're under no obligation to share anything."[67]

Oversharing is a significant problem in the digital age. It has led to the loss of personal privacy, destroyed friendships, and caused public humiliation—both for those who overshare about themselves and for those victimized by the oversharing of others. Remaining calm, thoughtful, and intentional about posting online can mitigate many of the negative effects of posting too much information. Just as digital literacy can help internet users distinguish good information from bad, make sense of the massive amounts of data at their fingertips, and avoid being scammed by schemes designed to part them from their money, digital literacy skills can help ensure that people post wisely—or do not post at all.

SOURCE NOTES

Introduction: Digital Literacy

1. The Onion, "High Cost of Childcare Forcing More Toddlers to Work Their Way Through Preschool," March 3, 2023. www.theonion.com.
2. Babylon Bee, "Banks Begin Calling Customers to Ask for Loans," March 22, 2023. https://babylonbee.com.
3. David French, "Hands off the Babylon Bee," *National Review*, July 30, 2019. www.nationalreview.com.
4. Quoted in Brett Samuels, "Trump Shares Fake Story from Satire Website to Criticize Twitter," *The Hill* (Washington, DC), October 16, 2020. https://thehill.com.
5. R. Kelly Garrett et al., "Too Many People Think Satirical News Is Real," The Conversation, August 16, 2019. https://theconversation.com.
6. Liana Loewus, "What Is Digital Literacy?," Education Week, November 8, 2016. www.edweek.org.
7. Center for the Future of Libraries, "Digital Natives." www.ala.org.

Chapter One: Making Sense of the Digital World

8. Seminole State College, "Research Foundations: Evaluate Information," June 21, 2022. https://libguides.seminolestate.edu.
9. Western Kentucky University, "Evaluating Websites," March 6, 2023. https://libguides.wku.edu.
10. Central Michigan University, "Website Research: URLs," December 22, 2022. https://libguides.cmich.edu.
11. UTEP Connect, "4 Ways to Differentiate a Good Source from a Bad Source," University of Texas at El Paso. www.utep.edu.
12. KK Rumrill, "Preventing Information Overload—Using Study Portals to Engage Site Staff," Clinical Leader, March 2, 2020. www.clinicalleader.com.
13. Neil Gaiman, "134th Commencement," University of the Arts, May 17, 2012. www.uarts.edu.

14. Rumrill, "Preventing Information Overload—Using Study Portals to Engage Site Staff."
15. Quoted in Cleveland Clinic, "Why Multitasking Doesn't Work," March 10, 2021. https://health.clevelandclinic.org.
16. Quoted in NICM Health Research Institute, Western Sydney University, "How the Internet May Be Changing the Brain," ScienceDaily, June 5, 2019. www.sciencedaily.com.
17. Quoted in Becky Larson, "Preview: We're All ADHD—Social Media & Attention Disorders," SXTXState, February 20, 2015. https://sxtxstate.com.
18. Youssef Farchakh et al., "Video Game Addiction and Its Association with Memory, Attention and Learning Skills in Lebanese Children," BioMed Central, December 12, 2020. https://capmh.biomedcentral.com.
19. Gaiman, "134th Commencement."
20. Christopher Curley, "These Internet-Blocking Apps Keep Me from Getting Distracted on the Job—and They've Become Essential Tools in My Work Arsenal," Business Insider, April 10, 2019. www.businessinsider.com.

Chapter Two: Fake News and Misinformation

21. Quoted in CBS News, "Transcript: Dr. Anthony Fauci Discusses Coronavirus on *Face the Nation*, March 22, 2020," March 22, 2020. www.cbsnews.com.
22. Quoted in McKenzie Sadeghi, "Fact Check: The COVID-19 Pandemic Is Not a Hoax," *USA Today*, January 5, 2022. www.usatoday.com.
23. Quoted in Tiffany Hsu, "As Covid-19 Continues to Spread, So Does Misinformation About It," *New York Times*, December 28, 2022. www.nytimes.com.
24. Quoted in John Naughton, "Fake News About COVID-19 Can Be as Dangerous as the Virus," *The Guardian* (Manchester, UK), March 14, 2020. www.theguardian.com.
25. Quoted in Taylor Synclair Goethe, "War, Propaganda, and Misinformation: The Evolution of Fake News," *Reporter*, April 26, 2019. https://reporter.rit.edu.
26. Quoted in Katherine Tully McManus, "QAnon Goes to Washington: Two Supporters Win Seats in Congress," *Roll Call* (Washington, DC), November 5, 2020. https://rollcall.com.

27. Quoted in Nur Ibrahim, "Tina Turner Is Not Dead, Despite YouTube Death Hoax," Snopes, January 24, 2023. www.snopes.com.
28. Jayson DeMers, "59 Percent of You Will Share This Article Without Even Reading It," *Forbes*, August 8, 2016. www.forbes.com.
29. Quoted in Grant Gross, "Fake News Spreads Fast, but Don't Blame the Bots," Internet Society, March 21, 2018. www.internetsociety .org.
30. Quoted in Kimberly Nicolaus, "Why Is It Difficult to Distinguish Between Fake News and Real News?," Medium, April 20, 2021. https://medium.com.
31. Quoted in Kyle Cheney and Nicholas Wu, "The Jan. 6 Panel's on a Hot Streak Against Trump World. Now What?," *Politico*, January 31, 2022. www.politico.com.
32. SUNY Geneseo, "Elections and Politics Information: Ways to Avoid the Spread of False Info on Social Media." https://library.geneseo .edu.
33. St. Louis Community College, "Fake News & Misinformation: How to Spot and Verify," December 7, 2022. https://guides.stlcc.edu.
34. Quoted in Lisa Ercolano, "How to Spot 'Fake News' Online," HUB, December 5, 2022. https://hub.jhu.edu.
35. Quoted in Susie Allen, "Critical Consumers," *University of Chicago Magazine*, Winter 2023, p. 14.
36. Quoted in NJ.gov, "Governor Murphy Signs Bipartisan Legislation Establishing First in the Nation K–12 Information Literacy Education," January 4, 2023. www.nj.gov.
37. Quoted in Whitney Burney, "News Literacy 2023: What to Look Out for to Spot Fake News," WXYZ, January 24, 2023. www.wxyz.com.
38. Quoted in Syracuse University, "Fake News: Why People Believe, How It Spreads, and What You Can Do About It," February 8, 2021. https://ischool.syr.edu.

Chapter Three: Scams, Attacks, and Hazards of the Digital World

39. Quoted in Kate Briquelet and Emily Shugerman, "She Was 69. He Was Young, Hunky—and a Fraud," Daily Beast, August 21, 2022. www.thedailybeast.com.
40. Quoted in Briquelet and Shugerman, "She Was 69."
41. Quoted in NBC News, "Former Nigerian Scam Artist Speaks Out," October 8, 2022. www.nbcnews.com.

42. Quoted in Briquelet and Shugerman, "She Was 69."

43. Emma Fletcher, "Romance Scammers' Favorite Lies Exposed," Federal Trade Commission, February 9, 2023. www.ftc.gov.

44. North Carolina Department of Justice, "Nigerian Money Transfer Scams," 2020. https://ncdoj.gov.

45. Jeff Laughlin, "The Prince Is Back and He Still Needs Your Help Moving Some Money, Old Scams Are New Scams," IT Spotlight, Southern Illinois University, Edwardsville, March 15, 2021. www.siue.edu.

46. Quoted in Smart Social, "5 Experts Share How Predators Entice Teens and Tweens Online," August 5, 2021. https://smartsocial.com.

47. Quoted in Gant News, "Allegheny County Man Arrested in Internet Child Porn Sting," January 4, 2007. https://gantnews.com.

48. Quoted in Nellie Bowles and Michael H. Keller, "Video Games and Online Chats Are 'Hunting Grounds' for Sexual Predators," *New York Times*, December 7, 2019. www.nytimes.com.

49. Kansas Attorney General's Office, "Protect Yourself from Scams," 2012. https://ag.ks.gov.

50. Federal Trade Commission, "How to Recognize and Avoid Phishing Scams," 2022. https://consumer.ftc.gov.

51. Susan Tompor, "Amazon Prime Day 2020: Beware of These Online Shopping Scams," *Detroit Free Press*, October 12, 2020. www.freep.com.

Chapter Four: Oversharing and Online Privacy

52. Quoted in Merlyn Thomas, "Sanna Marin: Finland PM Partying Video Causes Backlash," BBC, August 19, 2022. www.bbc.com.

53. Quoted in Rhoda Kwan, "Does a World Leader Have a Right to Party? Finland's Young, Female PM Puts It to the Test," NBC News, August 27, 2022. www.nbcnews.com.

54. Quoted in Sanya Mansoor, "Finland's Prime Minister Is Under Fire After a Video of Her Partying Leaked Online," *Time*, August 18, 2022. https://time.com.

55. Domo, "Data Never Sleeps 10.0," 2022. www.domo.com.

56. Quoted in Susan Skelly, "Why Do People Overshare on Social Media?," *The Lighthouse*, March 26, 2021. https://lighthouse.mq.edu.au.

57. NileFM, "9 Celebrities Who Destroyed Their Careers with Unfortunate Social Media Posts," April 28, 2020. https://nilefm.com.

58. Quoted in Oliver Darcy, "Hundreds of Newspapers Drop 'Dilbert' Comic Strip After Racist Tirade from Creator Scott Adams," CNN, February 27, 2023. www.cnn.com.
59. Quoted in Alison Green, "Update: Is My Future Manager a Bigoted Jerk?," Ask a Manager, February 28, 2023. www.askamanager.org.
60. Quoted in Andrea Cavallier, "Daycare Worker Fired After Posting About Hating Children on Facebook," WPIX, April 30, 2015. https://pix11.com.
61. IdentityForce, "Social Media Privacy: Are You Guilty of Oversharing?," June 30, 2022. www.identityforce.com.
62. Quoted in Judith Martin et al., "Miss Manners: Posting Party Photos for People Who Weren't Invited to See," *Washington Post*, March 8, 2023. www.washingtonpost.com.
63. Martin et al., "Miss Manners."
64. u/itsleeee, "My Friend Posted an Unflattering Picture of Me on Facebook," Reddit, March 25, 2018. www.reddit.com.
65. Lotus Group, "Venting on Facebook: Just Part of Life or Bad Idea?," November 29, 2012. https://lotusgroup.biz.
66. Van-Hau Trieu and Vanessa Cooper, "Why Do People Overshare Online? 5 Expert Tips for Avoiding Social Media Scandal," TuneFM, September 6, 2022. www.tunefm.net.
67. Quoted in Seek Go Create, "Digital Marketing Services: How to Be Authentic, Creative, and Strategic with Meredith Kallaher," May 16, 2022. https://seekgocreate.com.

FOR FURTHER RESEARCH

Books

Ellen C. Carillo, *MLA Guide to Digital Literacy*. 2nd ed. New York: Modern Language Association of America, 2022.

Kathryn Hulick, *Media Literacy: Information and Disinformation*. San Diego: ReferencePoint, 2023.

Rodney H. Jones and Christoph A. Hafner, *Understanding Digital Literacies: A Practical Introduction*. 2nd ed. New York: Routledge, 2021.

Hal Marcovitz, *Media Bias: What Is It and Why Does It Matter?* San Diego: ReferencePoint, 2022.

Don Nardo, *Information Glut: Sorting the Good from the Bad*. San Diego: ReferencePoint, 2023.

Laura Nicosia and James F. Nicosia, eds., *Digital Literacy: Skills & Strategies*. Amenia, NY: Salem, 2022.

J.K. O'Sullivan, *Online Scams*. San Diego: Brightpoint, 2022.

Jeffrey D. Wilhelm et al., *Fighting Fake News*. Thousand Oaks, CA: Corwin, 2023.

Internet Sources

Kate Briquelet and Emily Shugerman, "She Was 69. He Was Young, Hunky—and a Fraud," *Daily Beast*, August 21, 2022. www.thedailybeast.com.

Jayson DeMers, "59 Percent of You Will Share This Article Without Even Reading It," *Forbes*, August 8, 2016. www.forbes.com.

Federal Trade Commission, "How to Recognize and Avoid Phishing Scams," September 2022. https://consumer.ftc.gov.

Tiffany Hsu, "As COVID-19 Continues to Spread, So Does Misinformation About It," *New York Times*, December 28, 2022. www.nytimes.com.

Eva M. Krockow, "Is the Google Effect Messing with Your Brain?," *Stretching Theory* (blog), *Psychology Today*, September 8, 2021. www.psychologytoday.com.

Kimberly Nicolaus, "Why Is It Difficult to Distinguish Between Fake News and Real News?," Medium, April 20, 2021. https://medium.com.

Merlyn Thomas, "Sanna Marin: Finland PM Partying Video Causes Backlash," BBC, August 19, 2022. www.bbc.com.

Van-Hau Trieu and Vanessa Cooper, "Why Do People Overshare Online? 5 Expert Tips for Avoiding Social Media Scandal," TuneFM, September 6, 2022. www.tunefm.net.

Western Kentucky University, "Evaluating Websites," March 6, 2023. https://libguides.wku.edu.

Websites

American Library Association (ALA)
www.ala.org
The ALA focuses on providing library and information services, including material obtainable through the internet. The site provides resources to help internet users determine the accuracy and trustworthiness of various websites.

American Psychological Association (APA)
www.apa.org
The APA is an organization of psychologists. The resources it provides include information about the potentially damaging effects of overuse of the internet and oversharing online.

Federal Trade Commission (FTC)
www.ftc.gov
The FTC is a government agency. Its responsibilities include protecting American consumers from fraud, including internet-based swindles. Its website includes advice and fact sheets about online scams.

Snopes
www.snopes.com
Snopes is a fact-checking site that determines the validity of various claims, especially ones made online. The site does extensive research to identify falsehoods and fake news.

Washington Post Fact Checker
www.washingtonpost.com/news/fact-checker
Run by one of the nation's largest and most influential newspapers, this fact-checker investigates the accuracy of rumors and statements that commonly appear on the internet.

INDEX

Note: Boldface page numbers indicate illustrations.

Adams, Scott, 47, 50
advance-fee emails, 33, 36
Agarwal, Anish, 21
Aguilar, Pete, 26
American Library Association (ALA), 5, 29, 59
American Psychological Association (APA), 13, 59
Aral, Sinan, 25
Ask a Manager (website), 47
authorship, determining, 11–12

Babylon Bee (satirical news site), 4
Banks, Azealia, 46
Better Business Bureau, 34, 40
Biden, Joe, 4, 23
Bieber, Justin, 45
Boag, Simon, 45
Bolt, Usain, 24
Borowitz Report (satirical news site), 4
burglary, oversharing on social media and, 45
Business Insider, 18

Carrigan, Joe, 28
celebrities
  false rumors of deaths of, 23–24
  offensive comments by, 46–47

oversharing and, 44–15, 45–47
Center for Media Literacy, 30
Cleveland *Plain Dealer* (newspaper), 47
cognitive functioning
  benefits of internet on, 14
  negative impacts of social media interactions on, 11
Cold Turkey Blocker (website-blocking app), 18
Cooper, Vanessa, 52
COVID-19 pandemic/vaccine, 19–20, **20**, 21
  consequences of fake news on, 25–26
Curley, Christopher, 18
cyberbullying, 48, 50
Cyrus, Miley, 45, **46**

"Data Never Sleeps" (infographic), 44
digital literacy
  components of, 44
  critical thinking and, 5–7
  difficulty in identifying satirical news and, 4–5
  Google results from search on, 8
  information glut as obstacle to, 9
  limiting posts and, 52
  as protection from scammers/predators, 6–7, 40, 41
  success of online scams and increase in, 34

60

Domo (software company), 44

eBay (online shopping site), 40
email
  advance-fee scams by, 33, 36
  distractions from, 17–18

Facebook (social media platform)
  number of posts to, 44
  venting on, 50
FactCheck.org, 29
fake news
  appeal of, 27
  of celebrity deaths, 23–24
  on COVID-19, 21
  mainstream media coverage as
    indicator of, 27
  organizations combating,
    29–30
  political, in history, 21–23
  on 2020 presidential election,
    23
  role of schools/libraries in
    combating, 28–30
role of social media in spreading,
  24–26
Fauci, Anthony, 19
Federal Trade Commission (FTC),
  34, 41, 59
Firth, Joseph, 15
Fox News, 28
Francis, Laura, 31–32, 34
Freedom (website-blocking app),
  18
French, David, 4

Gaiman, Neil, 13, 17–18
Ghebreyesus, Tedros Adhanom,
  21
Google effect, 16
Green, Alison, 47

Greene, Marjorie Taylor, 23

Hajer, Braden, 28
Hearst, William Randolph, 22, 23
Hemsley, Jeff, 30
hoaxes, about COVID-19, 20–21
Hodge, Davidson, 31–32

IdentityForce (website), 48–49
information
  distinguishing good from bad,
    9–12
  Google effect and difficulty in
    remembering, 16
  internet and ease of obtaining,
    8–9
information glut
  biological/psychological
    impacts of, 12–13
  impact on memory, 15–16
  as obstacle to digital literacy, 9
Instagram (social media platform),
  44, 47
  number of posts to, 44
internet
  cognitive benefits of, 14
  ease of obtaining information
    on, 8–9
  tracking time spent on, 17
internet scams
  advance-fee, average loss from,
    36
  online shopping, 40
IQVIA Technologies, 13

January 6 insurrection (US
  Capitol, 2021), **24**, 26
Jeglic, Elizabeth, 38
Johns Hopkins Coronavirus
  Resource Center, 20
Jonas, Uschi, 26

Kallaher, Meredith, 52
Kardashian, Kim, 45
Kid, Rock, 24
Kubu, Cynthia, 14

Laughlin, Jeff, 36
Lawson, Matthew Asher, 27
Lincoln, Abraham, 22
Loewus, Liana, 5
Lokka, Tiina, 42

mainstream media
  coverage on, as indicator of
    fake news, 27
  satirical news sites
    masquerading as, 4, 24–25
Malik, Zayn, 46
malware (malicious software),
  37–38
Marin, Sanna, 42–44, **43**, 44,
  50
media literacy
  organizations encouraging,
    29–30
  states bringing into classroom,
    22
memory
  information glut and, 15–16
  internet use and, 14
  video gaming and, 17
Miss Manners, 49
Monmouth University, 23
Morant, Ja, 47, 50
multitasking, 17
Murphy, Phil, 28–29

National Association for Media
  Literacy Education, 29–30
National Institutes of Health, 16
Nesi, Jacqueline, 11
Nigerian letter scam, 36

Onion (satirical news site), 4
opinion polls. *See* surveys
oversharing, on social media,
  44, 45
  burglaries linked to, 45
  interpersonal issues and,
    49
  risks of, 44–45

phishing, 36–37
Pietrus, Michael, 15
polls. *See* surveys
Ponzi, Charles, 33
Ponzi schemes, 33–34
post sharing
  interrupting reflex to, 26–27
  of news articles without first
    opening, 25
  See also oversharing
predators, 38–39
presidential election of 2020,
  fake news on, 23, 26
Prinstein, Mitch, 11
Pritzker, J.B., 28
privacy
  case of Finnish prime minister,
    42–43
  harassment and, 48
  jobs/job loss and, 47–49
  oversharing and, 49, 51–52
  social media and, 44

QAnon (conspiracy theory), 23

Reddit (social media platform),
  49
  venting on, 50
RescueTime (website), 17
romantic fraud, 34–36
Ronaldo, Cristiano, 45
Roosevelt, Franklin D., 22

satirical news sites, 4
  difficulty in identifying, 5–6
scams
  advance-fee fraud, 33, 36
  malware, 37–38
  online shopping, 40
  phishing, 36–37
  Ponzi schemes, 33–34
  rise in, 34
  romance, 31–32, 34–35
sexual predators, 38–39
Snapchat (social media platform), 17, 18, 52
  oversharing on, 45
Snoop Dogg, 45
Snopes (website), 59
social media
  avoiding distractions from, 17–18
  permanence of postings on, 50
  risks of oversharing on, 45
Spone, Raffaela, 48
stress, 13–14
Sundar, S. Shyam, 27
SUNY Geneseo, 26
surveys
  on employers checking applicants' social media, 47
  on loss of friendships after posting, 49
  on loss of privacy on social media, 51
  on 2020 presidential election, 23

on recognizing satirical news, 4–5

TikTok (social media platform), 5, 17, 48
  policy on erroneous information, 30
Tompor, Susan, 41
Trieu, Van-Hau, 52
Trump, Donald, 4, 23
Turner, Tina, 23–24
Twitter (social media platform), 4, 52
  number of posts to, 44

University of Texas at El Paso, 12
Uso, Jey, 24

Victory Vipers (cheerleading team), 48
video games, 16–17

Washington Post Fact Checker (website), 59
West, Jevin, 22
Wright, Matt, 39

YouTube (social media platform), 5, 23
  number of videos uploaded to, 8, 44
  oversharing on, 45
  scamming on, 31–32
  spread of malware on, 38

PICTURE CREDITS

Cover: Vasya Kobelev/Shutterstock

6: Ground Picture/Shutterstock

10: Thaspol Sangsee/Shutterstock

12: Robert Daly/iStock

16: aslysun/Shutterstock

20: Ringo Chiu/Shutterstock

24: Sebastian Portillo/Shutterstock

29: Associated Press

35: Studio Romantic/Shutterstock

37: FellowNeko/Shutterstock

39: OWL_VISION_STUDIO/Shutterstock

43: Alexandros Michailidis/Shutterstock

46: Tinseltown/Shutterstock

51: Motortion Films/Shutterstock